CHRISTMAS IN POETRY

CHRISTMAS IN POETRY

VARIOUS,
CARNEGIE LIBRARY SCHOOL ASSOCIATION

ISBN: 978-93-5614-024-0

Published: 1922

LECTOR HOUSE LLP
E-MAIL: lectorpublishing@gmail.com

CHRISTMAS IN POETRY
CAROLS AND POEMS

CHOSEN BY A COMMITTEE
OF THE CARNEGIE LIBRARY SCHOOL ASSOCIATION

FIRST SERIES

1922

CONTENTS

Page

A CHRISTMAS CAROL

God bless the master of this house,
The mistress also,
And all the little children,
That round the table go.

And all your kin and folk,
That dwell both far and near;
I wish you a merry Christmas,
And a happy New Year.

Old English Carol

FROM FAR AWAY

From far away we come to you.
The snow in the street, and the wind on the door,
To tell of great tidings, strange and true.
Minstrels and maids, stand forth on the floor.
From far away we come to you,
To tell of great tidings, strange and true.

For as we wandered far and wide,
The snow in the street, and the wind on the door,
What hap do you deem there should us betide?
Minstrels and maids, stand forth on the floor.

Under a bent when the night was deep,
The snow in the street, and the wind on the door,
There lay three shepherds, tending their sheep.
Minstrels and maids, stand forth on the floor.

"O ye shepherds, what have ye seen,
The snow in the street, and the wind on the door,
To stay your sorrow and heal your teen?"
Minstrels and maids, stand forth on the floor.

"In an ox stall this night we saw,
The snow in the street, and the wind on the door,
A Babe and a maid without a flaw.
Minstrels and maids, stand forth on the floor.

"There was an old man there beside;
The snow in the street, and the wind on the door,
His hair was white, and his hood was wide.
Minstrels and maids, stand forth on the floor.

"And as we gazed this thing upon,
The snow in the street, and the wind on the door,
Those twain knelt down to the little one.
Minstrels and maids, stand forth on the floor.

"And a marvellous song we straight did hear,
The snow in the street, and the wind on the door.
That slew our sorrow and healed our care."
Minstrels and maids, stand forth on the floor.

News of a fair and marvellous thing,
The snow in the street, and the wind on the door,

Nowell, Nowell, Nowell, we sing.
Minstrels and maids, stand forth on the floor.
From far away we come to you,
To tell of great tidings, strange and true.

William Morris

LORDINGS, LISTEN TO OUR LAY

Lordings, listen to our lay—
We have come from far away
To seek Christmas;
In this mansion we are told
He His yearly feast doth hold:
'Tis to-day!
May joy come from God above,
To all those who Christmas love.

Old Carol

'TWAS JOLLY, JOLLY WAT

'Twas jolly, jolly Wat, my foy,
He was a goodman's shepherd boy,
And he sat by his sheep
On the hill-side so steep,
And piped this song,
Ut hoy! Ut hoy!
O merry, merry sing for joy,
Ut hoy!

A'down from Heav'n that is so high
There came an angel companye,
And on Bethlehem hill
Thro' the night-tide so still
Their song out-rang:
On high, On high,
O glory be to God on high,
On high!

Now must Wat go where Christ is born,
Yea, go and come again to-morn.
And my pipe it shall play,
All my heart it doth say
To Shepherd King:
Ut hoy! Ut hoy!
O merry, merry sing for joy,
Ut hoy!

O peace on earth, good will to men,
The angels sang again, again,
For to you was He born
On this Christmas morn,
So sing we all:
On high, On high,
O glory be to God on high,
On high!

Jesu my King, it's naught for Thee,
A bob of cherries, one, two, three,
But my tar-box and ball,
And my pipe, I give all
To Thee, my King.
Ut hoy! Ut hoy!

O merry, merry sing for joy,
Ut hoy!

Farewell, herd-boy, saith Mary mild.
Thanks, jolly Wat, smiled Mary's child,
For fit gift for a king
Is your heart in the thing.
So pipe you well,
For joy, for joy!
O merry, merry sing for joy,
Ut hoy!

C. W. Stubbs

BOOTS AND SADDLES

Our shepherds all
As pilgrims have departed,
Our shepherds all
Have gone to Bethlehem.
They gladly go
For they are all stout-hearted,
They gladly go—
Ah, could I go with them!

I am too lame to walk,
Boots and saddles, boots and saddles,
I am too lame to walk,
Boots and saddles, mount and ride.

A shepherd stout
Who sang a catamiaulo,
A shepherd stout
Was walking lazily.
He heard me speak
And saw me hobbling after,
He turned and said
He would give help to me.

"Here is my horse
That flies along the high-road,
Here is my horse,
The best in all the towns.
I bought him from
A soldier in the army,
I got my horse
By payment of five crowns."

When I have seen
The Child, the King of Heaven,
When I have seen
The Child who is God's son,
When to the mother,
I my praise have given,
When I have finished,
All I should have done:

No more shall I be lame,

Boots and saddles, boots and saddles,
No more shall I be lame,
Boots and saddles, mount and ride.

Provençal Noël of Nicholas Saboly

Included by permission of The H. W. Gray Company.

CAROL

Villagers all, this frosty tide,
Let your doors swing open wide,
Though wind may follow, and snow beside,
Yet draw us in by your fire to bide;
Joy shall be yours in the morning!

Here we stand in the cold and the sleet,
Blowing fingers and stamping feet,
Come from far away you to greet—
You by the fire and we in the street—
Bidding you joy in the morning!

For ere one half of the night was gone,
Sudden a star has led us on,
Raining bliss and benison—
Bliss to-morrow and more anon,
Joy for every morning!

Goodman Joseph toiled through the snow—
Saw the star o'er a stable low;
Mary she might not further go—
Welcome thatch, and litter below!
Joy was hers in the morning!

And then they heard the angels tell
"Who were the first to cry NOWELL?
Animals all, as it befell,
In the stable where they did dwell!
Joy shall be theirs in the morning!"

Kenneth Grahame

THE NEIGHBORS OF BETHLEHEM

Good neighbor, tell me why that sound,
That noisy tumult rising round,
Awaking all in slumber lying?
Truly disturbing are these cries,
All through the quiet village flying,
O come ye shepherds, wake, arise!

What, neighbor, then do ye not know
God hath appeared on earth below
And now is born in manger lowly!
In humble guise he came this night,
Simple and meek, this infant holy,
Yet how divine in beauty bright.

Good neighbor, I must make amend,
Forthwith to bring Him will I send,
And Joseph with the gentle Mother.
When to my home these three I bring,
Then will it far outshine all other,
A palace fair for greatest king!

Thirteenth Century French Carol

Included by permission of The H. W. Gray Company.

CAROL OF THE RUSSIAN CHILDREN

Snow-bound mountains, snow-bound valleys,
Snow-bound plateaus, clad in white,
Fur-robed moujiks, fur-robed nobles,
Fur-robed children, see the light.
Shaggy pony, shaggy oxen,
Gentle shepherds wait the light;
Little Jesus, little Mother,
Good St. Joseph, come this night.

Russian Folk Song

Included by permission of The H. W. Gray Company.

SIGNS OF CHRISTMAS

When on the barn's thatch'd roof is seen
The moss in tufts of liveliest green;
When Roger to the wood pile goes,
And, as he turns, his fingers blows;
When all around is cold and drear,
Be sure that Christmas-tide is near.

When up the garden walk in vain
We seek for Flora's lovely train;
When the sweet hawthorn bower is bare,
And bleak and cheerless is the air;
When all seems desolate around,
Christmas advances o'er the ground.

When Tom at eve comes home from plough,
And brings the mistletoe's green bough,
With milk-white berries spotted o'er,
And shakes it the sly maids before,
Then hangs the trophy up on high,
Be sure that Christmas-tide is nigh.

When Hal, the woodman, in his clogs,
Bears home the huge unwieldy logs,
That, hissing on the smouldering fire,
Flame out at last a quiv'ring spire;
When in his hat the holly stands,
Old Christmas musters up his bands.

When cluster'd round the fire at night,
Old William talks of ghost and sprite,
And, as a distant out-house gate
Slams by the wind, they fearful wait,
While some each shadowy nook explore,
Then Christmas pauses at the door.

When Dick comes shiv'ring from the yard,
And says the pond is frozen hard,
While from his hat, all white with snow,
The moisture, trickling, drops below,
While carols sound, the night to cheer,
Then Christmas and his train are here.

Edwin Lees

A CHRISTMAS HYMN

Once in royal David's city
Stood a lowly cattle-shed
Where a mother laid her Baby,
In a manger for His bed.
Mary was that mother mild,
Jesus Christ her little Child.

He came down to earth from heaven,
Who is God and Lord of all,
And His shelter was a stable,
And His cradle was a stall.
With the poor, and mean, and lowly
Lived on earth our Saviour holy.

And through all His wondrous childhood,
He would honour and obey.
Love and watch the lowly mother
In whose gentle arms He lay.
Christian children, all must be
Mild, obedient, good as He.

For He is our childhood's Pattern,
Day by day like us He grew;
He was little, weak, and helpless,
Tears and smiles like us He knew:
And He feeleth for our sadness,
And He shareth in our gladness.

And our eyes at last shall see Him,
Through His own redeeming love,
For that Child so dear and gentle
Is our Lord in Heaven above;
And He leads His children on
To the place where He is gone.

Not in that poor lowly stable,
With the oxen standing by,
We shall see Him; but in Heaven,
Set at God's right hand on high;
When like stars His children crowned,
All in white shall wait around.

C. Frances Alexander

CHRISTMAS

While shepherds watch'd their flocks by night,
All seated on the ground,
The angel of the Lord came down,
And glory shone around.

"Fear not," said he (for mighty dread
Had seized their troubled mind);
"Glad tidings of great joy I bring
To you and all mankind.

"To you, in David's town, this day
Is born of David's line
The Saviour who is Christ the Lord;
And this shall be the sign:

"The heavenly Babe you there shall find
To human view display'd,
All meanly wrapt in swathing bands,
And in a manger laid."

Thus spake the Seraph; and forthwith
Appear'd a shining throng
Of angels, praising God, and thus
Address'd their joyful song:

"All glory be to God on high,
And to the earth be peace;
Good-will henceforth from heaven to men
Begin, and never cease!"

Nahum Tate

THE STORY OF THE SHEPHERD

It was the very noon of night: the stars above the fold,
More sure than clock or chiming bell, the hour of midnight told:
When from the heav'ns there came a voice, and forms were seen to shine
Still bright'ning as the music rose with light and love divine.
With love divine, the song began; there shone a light serene:
O, who hath heard what I have heard, or seen what I have seen?

O ne'er could nightingale at dawn salute the rising day
With sweetness like that bird of song in his immortal lay:
O ne'er were woodnotes heard at eve by banks with poplar shade
So thrilling as the concert sweet by heav'nly harpings made;
For love divine was in each chord, and filled each pause between:
O, who hath heard what I have heard, or seen what I have seen?

I roused me at the piercing strain, but shrunk as from the ray
Of summer lightning: all around so bright the splendour lay.
For oh, it mastered sight and sense, to see that glory shine,
To hear that minstrel in the clouds, who sang of Love Divine,
To see that form with bird-like wings, of more than mortal mien:
O, who hath heard what I have heard, or seen what I have seen?

When once the rapturous trance was past, that so my sense could bind,
I left my sheep to Him whose care breathed in the western wind:
I left them, for instead of snow, I trod on blade and flower,
And ice dissolved in starry rays at morning's gracious hour,
Revealing where on earth the steps of Love Divine had been:
O, who hath heard what I have heard, or seen what I have seen?

I hasted to a low-roofed shed, for so the Angel bade;
And bowed before the lowly rack where Love Divine was laid:
A new-born Babe, like tender Lamb, with Lion's strength there smiled;
For Lion's strength immortal might, was in that new-born Child;
That Love Divine in child-like form had God for ever been:
O, who hath heard what I have heard, or seen what I have seen?

Translated from the Spanish

A CHRISTMAS CAROL

When Christ was born in Bethlehem,
'Twas night but seemed the noon of day:
The star whose light
Was pure and bright,
Shone with unwav'ring ray;
But one bright star,
One glorious star
Guided the Eastern Magi from afar.

Then peace was spread throughout the land;
The lion fed beside the lamb;
And with the kid,
To pastures led,
The spotted leopard fed
In peace, in peace
The calf and bear,
The wolf and lamb reposed together there.

As shepherds watched their flocks by night,
An angel brighter than the sun
Appeared in air,
And gently said,
"Fear not, be not afraid,
Behold, behold,
Beneath your eyes,
Earth has become a smiling Paradise."

Translated from the Neapolitan

THE GOLDEN CAROL

(Of Melchior, Balthazar, and Caspar, the Three Kings)

We saw the light shine out a-far,
On Christmas in the morning.
And straight we knew Christ's Star it was,
Bright beaming in the morning.
Then did we fall on bended knee,
On Christmas in the morning,
And prais'd the Lord, who'd let us see
His glory at its dawning.

Oh! every thought be of His Name,
On Christmas in the morning,
Who bore for us both grief and shame,
Afflictions sharpest scorning.
And may we die (when death shall come),
On Christmas in the morning,
And see in heav'n, our glorious home,
The Star of Christmas morning.

Old Carol

CHRISTMAS EVE

In holly hedges starving birds
Silently mourn the setting year;
Upright like silver-plated swords
The flags stand in the frozen mere.

The mistletoe we still adore
Upon the twisted hawthorn grows:
In antique gardens hellebore
Puts forth its blushing Christmas rose.

Shrivell'd and purple, cheek by jowl,
The hips and haws hang drearily;
Roll'd in a ball the sulky owl
Creeps far into his hollow tree.

In abbeys and cathedrals dim
The birth of Christ is acted o'er;
The kings of Cologne worship him,
Balthazar, Jasper, Melchior.

The shepherds in the field at night
Beheld an angel glory-clad.
And shrank away with sore afright.
"Be not afraid," the angel bade.

"I bring good news to king and clown,
To you here crouching on the sward;
For there is born in David's town
A Saviour, which is Christ the Lord.

"Behold the babe is swathed, and laid
Within a manger." Straight there stood
Beside the angel all arrayed
A heavenly multitude.

"Glory to God," they sang; "and peace,
Good pleasure among men."
The wondrous message of release!
Glory to God again!

Hush! Hark! the waits, far up the street!
A distant, ghostly charm unfolds,
Of magic music wild and sweet,
Anemones and clarigolds.

John Davidson

From "Fleet Street Eclogues." Included by permission of Dodd, Mead and Company.

CAROL OF THE BIRDS

Whence comes this rush of wings afar.
Following straight the Noël star?
Birds from the woods in wondrous flight,
Bethlehem seek this Holy Night.

"Tell us, ye birds, why come ye here.
Into this stable, poor and drear?"
"Hast'ning we seek the new-born King,
And all our sweetest music bring."

Hark how the green-finch bears his part,
Philomel, too, with tender heart,
Chants from her leafy dark retreat
Re, mi, fa, sol, in accents sweet.

Angels and shepherds, birds of the sky,
Come where the Son of God doth lie;
Christ on the earth with man doth dwell.
Join in the shout, Noël, Noël.

Bas-Quercy

THE SHEPHERDS HAD AN ANGEL

The shepherds had an angel,
The wise men had a star;
But what have I, a little child,
To guide me home from far,
Where glad stars sing together,
And singing angels are?

Lord Jesus is my Guardian,
So I can nothing lack;
The lambs lie in His bosom
Along life's dangerous track:
The wilful lambs that go astray
He, bleeding, brings them back.

Those shepherds thro' the lonely night
Sat watching by their sheep,
Until they saw the heav'nly host
Who neither tire nor sleep,
All singing Glory, glory,
In festival they keep.

Christ watches me, His little lamb,
Cares for me day and night,
That I may be His own in heav'n;
So angels clad in white
Shall sing their Glory, glory,
For my sake in the height.

Lord, bring me nearer day by day,
Till I my voice unite,
And sing my Glory, glory,
With angels clad in white.
All Glory, glory, giv'n to Thee,
Thro' all the heav'nly height.

Christina G. Rossetti

SONG OF A SHEPHERD BOY
AT BETHLEHEM

Sleep, Thou little Child of Mary,
Rest Thee now.
Though these hands be rough from shearing
And the plow,
Yet they shall not ever fail Thee,
When the waiting nations hail Thee,
Bringing palms unto their King.
Now—I sing.

Sleep, Thou little Child of Mary,
Hope divine.
If Thou wilt but smile upon me,
I will twine
Blossoms for Thy garlanding.
Thou'rt so little to be King,
God's Desire!
Not a brier
Shall be left to grieve Thy brow;
Rest Thee now.

Sleep, Thou little Child of Mary,
Some fair day
Wilt Thou, as Thou wert a brother,
Come away
Over hills and over hollow?
All the lambs will up and follow.
Follow but for love of Thee.
Lov'st Thou me?

Sleep, Thou little Child of Mary,
Rest Thee now.
I that watch am come from sheep-stead
And from plough.
Thou wilt have disdain of me
When Thou'rt lifted, royally,
Very high for all to see:
Smilest Thou?

Josephine Preston Peabody

Included by permission of the author.

THE LEAST OF CAROLS

Loveliest dawn of gold and rose
Steals across undrifted snows;
In brown, rustling oak leaves stir
Squirrel, nuthatch, woodpecker;
Brief their matins, but, by noon,
All the sunny wood's a-tune:
Jays, forgetting their harsh cries,
Pipe a spring note, clear and true;
Wheel on angel wings of blue,
Trumpeters of Paradise;
Then the tiniest feathered thing,
All a-flutter, tail and wing,
Gives himself to caroling:

"Chick-a-dee-dee, chick-a-dee!
Jesulino, hail to thee!
Lowliest baby born to-day,
Pillowed on a wisp of hay;
King no less of sky and earth,
And singing sea;
Jesu! Jesu! most and least!
For the sweetness of thy birth
Every little bird and beast,
Wind and wave and forest tree,
Praises God exceedingly,
Exceedingly."

Sophie Jewett

From "The Poems of Sophie Jewett." Included by permission of the Thomas Y. Crowell Company.

NATIVITY SONG

The beautiful mother is bending
Low where her baby lies,
Helpless and frail, for her tending;
But she knows the glorious eyes.

The mother smiles and rejoices
While the baby laughs in the hay;
She listens to heavenly voices:
"The child shall be king, one day."

O dear little Christ in the manger,
Let me make merry with thee.
O King, in my hour of danger,
Wilt thou be strong for me?

Adapted from the Latin of Jacopone da Todi by
Sophie Jewett

THE CHRISTMAS SILENCE

Hushed are the pigeons cooing low,
On dusty rafters of the loft;
And mild-eyed oxen, breathing soft,
Sleep on the fragrant hay below.

Dim shadows in the corner hide;
The glimmering lantern's rays are shed
Where one young lamb just lifts his head,
Then huddles 'gainst his mother's side.

Strange silence tingles in the air;
Through the half-open door a bar
Of light from one low hanging star
Touches a baby's radiant hair—

No sound—the mother, kneeling, lays
Her cheek against the little face.
Oh human love! Oh heavenly grace!
'Tis yet in silence that she prays!

Ages of silence end to-night;
Then to the long-expectant earth
Glad angels come to greet His birth
In burst of music, love, and light!

Margaret Deland

Included by permission of the author.

BRING A TORCH, JEANETTE, ISABELLA!

Bring a torch, Jeanette, Isabella!
Bring a torch, to the cradle run!
It is Jesus, good folk of the village;
Christ is born, and Mary's calling;
Ah! Ah! beautiful is the mother;
Ah! Ah! beautiful is her son.

It is wrong when the Child is sleeping,
It is wrong to talk so loud;
Silence, all, as you gather around,
Lest your noise should waken Jesus:
Hush! Hush! see how fast He slumbers;
Hush! Hush! see how fast He sleeps.

Who goes there a-knocking so loudly?
Who goes there a-knocking like that?
Ope your doors, I have here on a plate
Some very good cakes which I am bringing:
Toc! Toc! quickly your doors now open;
Toc! Toc! come let us make good cheer.

Softly to the little stable,
Softly for a moment come;
Look and see how charming is Jesus,
How He is white, His cheeks are rosy.
Hush! Hush! see how the Child is sleeping;
Hush! Hush! see how He smiles in dreams.

Provençal Noël of Nicholas Saboly

CHRISTMAS FOLKSONG

The little Jesus came to town;
The wind blew up, the wind blew down;
Out in the street the wind was bold.
Now who would house Him from the cold?

Then opened wide a stable door
Fain were the rushes on the floor;
The Ox put forth a horned head:
"Come, little Lord, here make Thy bed."

Uprose the Sheep were folded near:
"Thou Lamb of God, come, enter here."
He entered there to rush and reed,
Who was the Lamb of God indeed.

The little Jesus came to town;
With ox and sheep He laid Him down.
Peace to the byre, peace to the fold,
For that they housed Him from the cold.

Lisette Woodworth Reese

Included by permission of Thomas B. Mosher.

AS JOSEPH WAS A-WALKING

As Joseph was a-walking
He heard an angel sing:—
"This night there shall be born
Our heavenly King.

"He neither shall be born
In housen, nor in hall,
Nor in the place of Paradise,
But in an ox's stall.

"He neither shall be clothéd
In purple nor in pall;
But in the fair, white linen,
That usen babies all.

"He neither shall be rockéd
In silver nor in gold,
But in a wooden cradle
That rocks on the mould.

"He neither shall be christened
In white wine nor in red,
But with fair spring water
With which we were christenéd."

Mary took her baby,
She dressed Him so sweet,
She laid Him in a manger,
All there for to sleep.

As she stood over Him
She heard angels sing,
"O bless our dear Saviour,
Our heavenly King."

From the Cherry Tree Carol

CRADLE HYMN

Away in a manger, no crib for a bed,
The little Lord Jesus laid down his sweet head.
The stars in the bright sky looked down where he lay—
The little Lord Jesus asleep on the hay.

The cattle are lowing, the baby awakes,
But little Lord Jesus, no crying he makes.
I love thee, Lord Jesus! Look down from the sky,
And stay by my cradle till morning is nigh.

Martin Luther

A CHRISTMAS CAROL

In the bleak mid-winter
Frosty wind made moan,
Earth stood hard as iron,
Water like a stone;
Snow had fallen, snow on snow,
Snow on snow,
In the bleak mid-winter
Long ago.

Our God, Heaven cannot hold Him
Nor earth sustain;
Heaven and earth shall flee away
When He comes to reign.
In the bleak mid-winter
A stable-place sufficed
The Lord God Almighty
Jesus Christ.

Angels and archangels
May have gathered there,
Cherubim and seraphim
Thronged the air;
But only His Mother
In her maiden bliss
Worshipped her Beloved
With a kiss.

What can I give Him,
Poor as I am?
If I were a shepherd
I would bring a lamb,
If I were a Wise Man,
I would do my part, —
Yet what I can I give Him,
Give my heart.

Christina G. Rossetti

CAROL

When the herds were watching
In the midnight chill,
Came a spotless lambkin
From the heavenly hill.

Snow was on the mountains,
And the wind was cold,
When from God's own garden
Dropped a rose of gold.

When 'twas bitter winter,
Houseless and forlorn
In a star-lit stable
Christ the Babe was born.

Welcome, heavenly lambkin;
Welcome, golden rose;
Alleluia, Baby,
In the swaddling clothes!

William Canton

A CHILD'S PRESENT
TO HIS CHILD-SAVIOUR

Go, pretty child, and bear this flower
Unto thy little Saviour;
And tell Him, by that bud now blown,
He is the Rose of Sharon known.
When thou hast said so, stick it there
Upon His bib, or stomacher;
And tell Him, for good handsel[1] too,
That thou hast brought a whistle new,
Made of a clean straight oaten reed,
To charm his cries at time of need.
Tell Him, for coral thou hast none,
But if thou hadst, He should have one;
But poor thou art, and known to be
Even as moneyless as He.
Lastly, if thou canst win a kiss
From those mellifluous lips of His,
Then never take a second on,
To spoil the first impression.

Robert Herrick

---

[1] Handsel: a gift for good luck.

A CHRISTMAS CAROL

There's a song in the air!
There's a star in the sky!
There's a mother's deep prayer
And a baby's low cry!
And the star rains its fire while the Beautiful sing,
For the manger of Bethlehem cradles a king.

There's a tumult of joy
O'er the wonderful birth,
For the virgin's sweet boy
Is the Lord of the earth,
Ay! the star rains its fire and the Beautiful sing,
For the manger of Bethlehem cradles a king.

In the light of that star
Lie the ages impearled;
And that song from afar
Has swept over the world.
Every hearth is aflame, and the Beautiful sing
In the homes of the nations that Jesus is King.

We rejoice in the light,
And we echo the song
That comes down through the night
From the heavenly throng.
Ay! we shout to the lovely evangel they bring,
And we greet in His cradle our Saviour and King.

Josiah Gilbert Holland

THE SHEPHERD WHO STAYED

There are in Paradise
Souls neither great nor wise,
Yet souls who wear no less
The crown of faithfulness.

My master bade me watch the flock by night;
My duty was to stay. I do not know
What thing my comrades saw in that great light,
I did not heed the words that bade them go,
I know not were they maddened or afraid;
I only know I stayed.

The hillside seemed on fire; I felt the sweep
Of wings above my head; I ran to see
If any danger threatened these my sheep.
What though I found them folded quietly,
What though my brother wept and plucked my sleeve,
They were not mine to leave.

Thieves in the wood and wolves upon the hill,
My duty was to stay. Strange though it be,
I had no thought to hold my mates, no will
To bid them wait and keep the watch with me.
I had not heard that summons they obeyed;
I only know I stayed.

Perchance they will return upon the dawn
With word of Bethlehem and why they went.
I only know that watching here alone,
I know a strange content.
I have not failed that trust upon me laid;
I ask no more—I stayed.

Theodosia Garrison

Included by permission of the author and of The Century Company.

GOOD KING WENCESLAS

Good King Wenceslas looked out
On the Feast of Stephen,
When the snow lay round about,
Deep, and crisp, and even.

Brightly shone the moon that night
Though the frost was cruel,
When a poor man came in sight,
Gath'ring winter fuel.

"Hither, page, and stand by me,
If thou know'st it, telling.
Yonder peasant, who is he?
Where and what his dwelling?"

"Sire, he lives a good league hence,
Underneath the mountain;
Right against the forest fence,
By Saint Agnes' fountain."

"Bring me flesh, and bring me wine,
Bring me pine-logs hither;
Thou and I shall see him dine,
When we bear them thither."

Page and monarch, forth they went,
Forth they went together;
Through the rude wind's wild lament
And the bitter weather.

"Sire, the night is darker now,
And the wind blows stronger;
Fails my heart, I know not how,
I can go no longer."

"Mark my footsteps, good my page;
Tread thou in them boldly:
Thou shalt find the winter rage
Freeze thy blood less coldly."

In his master's steps he trod,
Where the snow lay dinted;
Heat was in the very sod
Where the saint has printed.

Therefore, Christian men, be sure,
Wealth or rank possessing,
Ye who now will bless the poor,
Shall yourselves find blessing.

Translated from the Latin by J. M. Neale

WE THREE KINGS

We Three Kings of Orient are,
Bearing gifts we traverse afar,
Field and fountain,
Moor and mountain,
Following yonder star.

Chorus
O Star of wonder, Star of night,
Star with Royal Beauty bright,
Westward leading.
Still proceeding,
Guide us to Thy perfect Light.

Gaspard: Born a king on Bethlehem plain,
Gold I bring to crown Him again;
King forever,
Ceasing never
Over us all to reign.

Chorus: O Star of wonder....

Melchior: Frankincense to offer have I,
Incense owns a deity nigh;
Prayer and praising
All men raising,
Worship Him God on high.

Chorus: O Star of wonder....

Balthazar: Myrrh is mine; its bitter perfume
Breathes a life of gathering gloom;
Sorrowing, sighing,
Bleeding, dying,
Sealed in a stone-cold tomb.

Chorus: O Star of wonder....

Glorious now behold Him arise,
King and God, and Sacrifice;
Heav'n sings Allelujah:
Allelujah,
The earth replies.

J. H. Hopkins, Jr.

GOD REST YE, MERRY GENTLEMEN

God rest ye, merry gentlemen; let nothing you dismay,
For Jesus Christ, our Saviour, was born on Christmas-day.
The dawn rose red o'er Bethlehem, the stars shone through the gray,
When Jesus Christ, our Saviour, was born on Christmas-day.

God rest ye, little children; let nothing you affright,
For Jesus Christ, your Saviour, was born this happy night;
Along the hills of Galilee the white flocks sleeping lay,
When Christ, the child of Nazareth, was born on Christmas-day.

God rest ye, all good Christians; upon this blessed morn
The Lord of all good Christians was of a woman born:
Now all your sorrows He doth heal, your sins He takes away;
For Jesus Christ, our Saviour, was born on Christmas-day.

Dinah Maria Mulock

THE WASSAIL SONG

Here we come a-wassailing
Among the leaves so green,
Here we come a-wandering
So fair to be seen.

Love and joy come to you
And to your wassail too,
And God bless you, and send you
A happy New Year.

We are not daily beggars
That beg from door to door,
But we are neighbours' children
That you have seen before.

Good Master and good Mistress,
As you sit by the fire,
Pray think of us poor children
Who are wandering in the mire.

Bring us out a table
And spread it with a cloth;
Bring us out a mouldy cheese
And some of your Christmas loaf.

God bless the master of this house,
Likewise the mistress too;
And all the little children
That round the table go.

Old Devonshire Carol

Included by permission of The H. W. Gray Company.

WASSAILER'S SONG

Wassail! Wassail! all over the town,
Our bread it is white, our ale it is brown;
Our bowl is made of a maplin tree;
We be good fellows all;—I drink to thee.

Here's to our horse, and to his right ear,
God send master a happy new year;
A happy new year as ever he did see,—
With my wassail bowl I drink to thee.

Here's to our mare, and to her right eye,
God send our mistress a good Christmas pie;
A good Christmas pie as e'er I did see,—
With my wassailing bowl I drink to thee.

Here's to our cow, and to her long tail,
God send our master us never may fail
Of a cup of good beer: I pray you draw near,
And our jolly wassail it's then you shall hear.

Be here any maids? I suppose here be some;
Sure they will not let young men stand on the cold stone!
Sing hey, O, maids! come trole back the pin,
And the fairest maid in the house let us all in.

Come, butler, come, bring us a bowl of the best;
I hope your souls in heaven will rest;
But if you do bring us a bowl of the small,
Then, down fall butler, and bowl and all.

Robert Southwell

CAROL IN PRAISE OF THE HOLLY AND IVY

(Holly and Ivy Made a Great Party)

Holly and Ivy made a great party,
Who should have the mastery
In lands where they go.

Then spake Holly, "I am fierce and jolly,
I will have the mastery
In lands where we go."

Then spake Ivy, "I am loud and proud,
And I will have the mastery
In lands where we go."

Then spake Holly, and bent him down on his knee,
"I pray thee, gentle Ivy,
Essay me no villany
In the lands where we go."

Fifteenth Century Carol

CEREMONIES FOR CHRISTMAS

Come, bring with a noise,
My merry, merry boys,
The Christmas log to the firing,
While my good dame, she
Bids ye all be free,
And drink to your heart's desiring.

With the last year's brand
Light the new block, and
For good success in his spending,
On your psalteries play,
That sweet luck may
Come while the log is a-tending.

Drink now the strong beer,
Cut the white loaf here,
The while the meat is a-shredding;
For the rare mince-pie
And the plums stand by
To fill the paste that's a-kneading.

Robert Herrick

CHRISTMAS EVE—ANOTHER CEREMONY

Come, guard this night the Christmas-pie,
That the thief, though ne'er so sly,
With his flesh-hooks, don't come nigh
To catch it.

From him, who alone sits there,
Having his eyes still in his ear,
And a deal of nightly fear
To watch it.

Robert Herrick

CHRISTMAS EVE—ANOTHER CEREMONY TO THE MAIDS

Wash your hands, or else the fire
Will not tend to your desire;
Unwashed hands, ye maidens, know,
Dead the fire, though ye blow.

Robert Herrick

OUR JOYFUL FEAST

So, now is come our joyful feast,
Let every soul be jolly!
Each room with ivy leaves is drest,
And every post with holly.
Though some churls at our mirth repine,
Round your brows let garlands twine,
Drown sorrow in a cup of wine,
And let us all be merry!

Now all our neighbours' chimneys smoke,
And Christmas logs are burning;
Their ovens with baked meats do choke,
And all their spits are turning.
Without the door let sorrow lie,
And if for cold it hap to die,
We'll bury it in Christmas pie,
And evermore be merry!

George Wither

Lector House believes that a society develops through a two-fold approach of continuous learning and adaptation, which is derived from the study of classic literary works spread across the historic timeline of literature records. Therefore, we aim at reviving, repairing and redeveloping all those inaccessible or damaged but historically as well as culturally important literature across subjects so that the future generations may have an opportunity to study and learn from past works to embark upon a journey of creating a better future.

This book is a result of an effort made by Lector House towards making a contribution to the preservation and repair of original ancient works which might hold historical significance to the approach of continuous learning across subjects.

HAPPY READING & LEARNING!

LECTOR HOUSE LLP
E-MAIL: lectorpublishing@gmail.com